TAYLOR SWIFT
ICON

Katy Sprinkel

TRIUMPH
BOOKS

Library of Congress Cataloging-in-Publication
Data is available upon request.

This book is available in quantity at special
discounts for your group or organization. For
further information, contact:

Triumph Books LLC
814 North Franklin Street
Chicago, Illinois 60610
(312) 337-0747
www.triumphbooks.com

Printed in U.S.A.

ISBN: 978-1-63727-486-6

Design by Patricia Frey
Edited by Laine Morreau

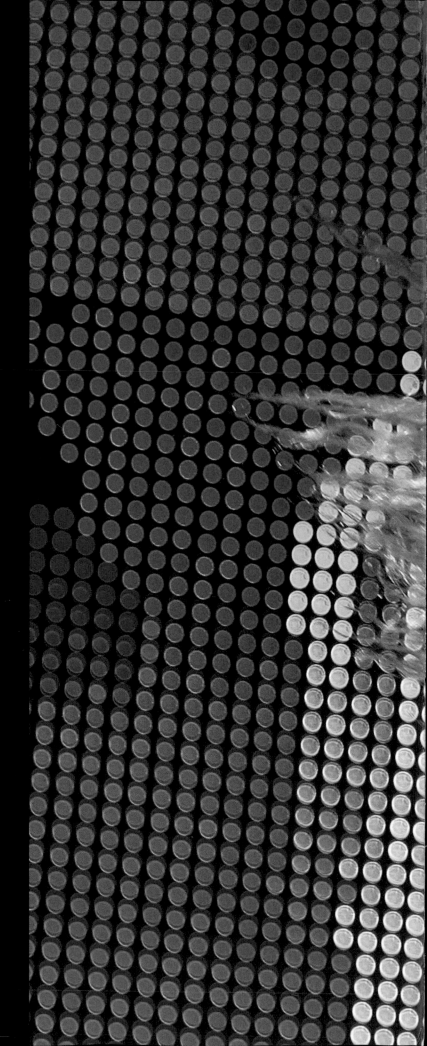

CONTENTS

Introduction
THE SUPERSTAR

Celebrating a third Grammy win for Album of the Year, this time for *Folklore* in 2021.

Taylor Swift is an artist at the top of her game, with a record-breaking album and an in-demand tour that has her poised to stage the most lucrative tour of all time. She has been around for so long, and been so successful, that it's easy to forget how many records she's already broken, awards she's garnered, and glass ceilings she's shattered. She's one of the biggest musical artists not just today but in history.

She's a consummate performer who sells out arenas around the globe. She's a prolific songwriter and musician with an uncanny knack for reinvention. She's an influencer who uses her immense platform for good, and a musician who lifts up others' talent wherever she sees it. She's a boss of the highest order, a multihyphenate who can seemingly do it all.

It was impossible to imagine what worlds she could possibly conquer that she hadn't already. And then came her 10th studio album, *Midnights*. With it, she did what no other artist had done in chart history: she simultaneously occupied *all 10 spots* in the Billboard Top 10. It's a credit to the Swifties, as her longtime and loyal fans refer to themselves. Swift's ability to pour her vulnerabilities into her music is the foundation of her connection with her audience, with whom she has a unique relationship.

This book explores 10 aspects of Taylor that make her an undisputed icon: Wunderkind. Creator. Mastermind. Innovator. Performer. Bestie. Advocate. Influencer. Fashionista. Overachiever. She is a singular talent and an artist doing it all on her own terms. This is her story. *Are you ready for it?* •

Taylor Swift performs onstage at the Prudential Center on March 29, 2013, in Newark, New Jersey.

Chapter One
THE WUNDERKIND

It was a banner year in 2007 for Taylor, as the accolades for her debut album, *Taylor Swift*, came rolling in. Here she accepts the CMT Award for best new artist.

Taylor Alison Swift was born on December 13, 1989, when uber-divas such as Madonna and Janet Jackson were dominating the charts. Perhaps it was inevitable that Taylor would one day join the ranks of pop divas in her own right. But she was named after '70s mainstay James Taylor, and she is every bit as much a singer-songwriter, like he was, as she is a pop star.

Her father, Scott, was a stockbroker, and her mother, Andrea, was a finance executive. Both of them had seen success in business and wanted Taylor to have every advantage to achieve her own goals. Giving her an androgynous name, they reasoned, would serve her well in life. "My mom thought it was cool that if you got a business card that said 'Taylor,' you wouldn't know if it was a guy or a girl," Taylor told *Rolling Stone* in 2009. "She wanted me to be a businessperson in a business world."

The Swifts lived on a sprawling 11-acre Christmas tree farm called Pine Ridge Farm, replete with roaming cats and a stable of seven horses. It was a seasonal side business for the Swift family, but for young Taylor, it was paradise. "[That] little farm," Swift remembered, "was the biggest place in the world. And it was the most magic, wonderful place in the world."

Taylor's brother, Austin, came along two years later, in 1992. Andrea left her career to become a full-time parent to Taylor and Austin, and the Swifts moved from the countryside into town in 1997. Home was the sleepy borough of Wyomissing, Pennsylvania, an affluent suburb of Reading.

Taylor's creativity shone from an early age, when she showed an aptitude for writing. At 10 she entered a national poetry contest and won it, for a long-form poem titled "Monster in My Closet." She also tried her hand at novel writing—an unusual pursuit for an elementary-aged child, to say the least. The words just seemed to flow out of her. "I think I fell in love with words before I fell in love with music," the singer recalled to NBC's Katie Couric. "All I wanted to do was talk, and all I wanted to do was hear stories."

12

After learning a handful of guitar chords from a visiting computer repairman (naturally!), Taylor wrote her first song at age 12. It was called "Lucky You." And lucky for everyone else that the Swifts had computer trouble!

Swift's family enrolled her in a local children's theater in grade school, and she even took acting and singing lessons in New York City, to which the family would also often make the two-and-a-half-hour drive to take in Broadway performances. She took to the theater naturally, and was cast as the lead in local productions, including as Sandy in *Grease*, Maria in *The Sound of Music*, and Kim in *Bye Bye Birdie*.

In singing, she found an avenue for self-expression that felt like home. A friend of her parents suggested she try her hand at country music when she was around 10, and something just clicked. It felt like the

> "Label executives in Nashville [told] me that only 35-year-old housewives listen to country music and there was no place for a 13-year-old on their roster."
>
> —TAYLOR TO NYU IN 2022

right fit. "I think I first realized I wanted to be in country music and be an artist when I was 10. And I started dragging my parents to festivals, and fairs, and karaoke contests," Swift told *American Songwriter*.

Keeping it in the family—with parents Scott and Andrea in 2013.

She had a stable of go-to tunes, but Taylor's favorite of them to perform was the Dixie Chicks' girl-power anthem "Goodbye Earl," a delicious revenge ballad about two loyal besties.

Young Taylor brought a competitive fire to everything she did, whether it was riding horses, writing stories, or singing. She scoured the papers looking for contests to enter and karaoke nights at which she could perform. One promising contest was held at the Pat Garrett Roadhouse in nearby Strausstown, Pennsylvania, and the grand prize winner would open for a major country act. (Garrett also owned a nearby concert venue, where many national country artists would play.) Taylor kept coming back, entering the contest nearly every week until, at age 11, she won it all—along with a prime gig opening for country music icon Charlie Daniels.

But winning karaoke contests to open for bigger acts was hardly the most efficient way to get herself in front of big crowds. The Swifts also helped Taylor book national anthem gigs; she started singing "The Star-Spangled Banner" at local athletic events, and soon graduated to some of Philadelphia's biggest sporting stages, including 76ers and Phillies games.

DID YOU KNOW?

Music does run in the blood. Taylor's maternal grandmother, Marjorie Finlay, was an internationally acclaimed opera singer. Taylor credits her with being the first and foremost inspiration for her singing career. "I think watching her get up in front of people every single week [in church] made me think it wasn't that big of a deal to get up in front of people," Taylor recalled. She paid tribute to her grandmother on the *Evermore* track "Marjorie," which includes backing vocals from the late Finlay.

Marjorie Finlay (née Moehlenkamp) in 1949. *Archival photo from Lindenwood University*

Chapter One
THE WUNDERKIND

Her talent was undeniable, and was only growing in size. Soon it became clear that she belonged on an even bigger stage, and she turned her sights to Nashville. The Swifts traveled to Music City, and Taylor literally started knocking on doors up and down Music Row while her mom sat outside waiting in the car. "I would say, 'Hi, I'm Taylor. I'm 11. I want a record deal. Call me,'" she told *Entertainment Weekly*. There were a lot of rejections, and she got a lot of wild advice, but she kept going.

She had the fire and the voice, but she knew she needed even more. Her family, in support of her dream, relocated to Hendersonville, Tennessee, about 20 miles from Nashville. She started learning the guitar and applying herself more diligently to the craft of songwriting. She played live whenever she could and tried to get in front of as many music-industry people as she could.

Her hard work and persistence eventually paid off, landing her a writing deal with Sony—becoming their youngest-ever songwriter at age 14—and a development deal with RCA Records to pursue her own record. But while she was over the moon to land the record deal she had long desired, she and RCA had

Singing the national anthem before the game between the Los Angeles Dodgers and the Colorado Rockies on Opening Day at Dodger Stadium on April 9, 2007.

divergent ideas. The most contentious among them was that the company wanted her to sing other artists' songs rather than her own. Bolstered by her progress with Sony as a writer and her belief in her own talent, she made the difficult decision to cancel the RCA deal.

Swift felt she had the whole package, and she wasn't alone. Soon after the RCA contract was dissolved, Taylor crossed paths with a producer named Scott Borchetta, who was launching his own record label, Big Machine Records. "It was a lightning bolt for me," Borchetta told *Billboard* in 2016, recalling their first meeting. He quickly moved to sign Taylor, putting her straight to work penning music for what would eventually become her freshman album, *Taylor Swift*.

Her debut single, "Tim McGraw," immediately put her on the map, landing her in the top 10 of the Billboard country charts when she was only 16 years old. What seemed like an overnight success story was anything but; rather, it was the product of years and years of grit and determination. And she was only just beginning. •

HITSTORY: "Tim McGraw"

Born out of the anguish of a broken teen relationship, the song is a heartfelt farewell to love lost. It may also be the only Billboard-charting song ever conceived during math class. "The concept for this song hit me because I was dating a guy who moved away, and it was going to be over for us," Taylor remembered to *The Boot*. "So I started thinking of things that I knew would remind him of me. The first thing that came to mind was that my favorite song is by Tim McGraw. After school, I went downtown, sat down at the piano, and wrote this with [cowriter] Liz Rose in 15 minutes," Swift continued. "It may be the best 15 minutes I've ever experienced."

Country superstars Tim McGraw and Faith Hill were both huge early influences on Taylor's career. The couple, shown here during rehearsals in 2018, guest-performed with Taylor on her Reputation tour.

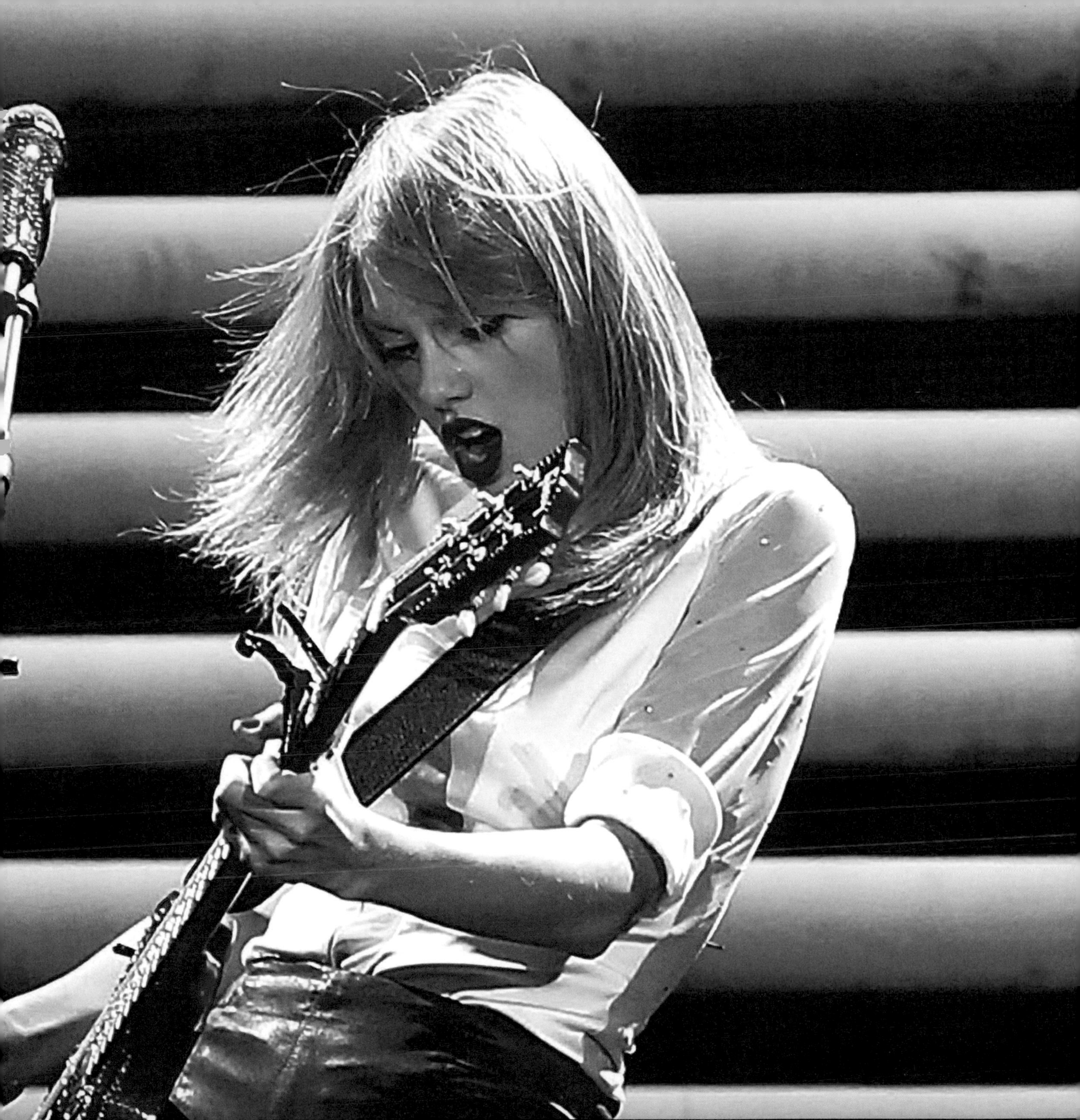

Chapter Two

THE CREATOR

Taylor performs the 10-minute version of "All Too Well" onstage during the 2022 NSAI Nashville Songwriter Awards.

There's a lot that goes into being a successful artist. And when you're as big as Taylor, the responsibilities that go along with being a megastar can pull you in a million different directions. For Taylor, songwriting is her home base and the one thing she's happiest doing.

"That's the purest part of my job," she told *Harper's Bazaar.* "It can get complicated on every other level, but the songwriting is still the same uncomplicated process it was when I was 12 years old."

Unlike many artists, she's not opaque about how she creates her music. On the contrary—she's extremely forthcoming with her fans, giving them incredible access into how her musical mind works. She often shares social media posts with glimpses of her creative process: videos, recorded voice memos, writing, and more.

She is an artist devoted to making the very best of her craft, bouncing ideas off the wall and seeing which ones stick. She'll change lyrics up at the last second, or

throw big chunks of a song out completely. She'll fret over a single word in the chorus, mulling it over and over until the delivery has *just* the right inflection. What comes across is the true joy of creation in all its messiness and chaos. "It's just fun. We're fully, fully acting on impulse. And we're acting on intuition and we're acting on excitement and oat milk lattes," she told the *New York Times* in 2022.

The idea for a song can come at any point, so Taylor has a couple bulletproof strategies for capturing the moment. At home or on the road, she's never far from a piano or a guitar, so she can work out melodies on the fly. Her other songwriting secret weapon? Her phone. When inspiration strikes, the first thing she'll usually do is grab her phone and record a voice memo of herself singing a hook or a piece of a melody. Or she'll tap out a stray lyric. She also uses her phone to store random ideas that don't have any context yet. An avid reader, she keeps lists of words that pique her interest, for

13

Forget triskaidekaphobia; 13 is Taylor's lucky number! "I was born on December 13th, I turned 13 on Friday the 13th, I [first] played on Jay Leno on February 13th. My album went gold in 13 weeks," Taylor told *Unrated* magazine in 2006. The list of lucky 13s goes on and on for Taylor—and so does her run of good luck!

Taylor poses with frequent collaborators Jack Antonoff (left) and Aaron Dessner (right) at the 2021 Grammys.

example. And she writes down snatches of conversation she hears out in the world and phrases that, with a little tweak, might just be the focus of a song someday. "Sometimes a string of words just ensnares me, and I can't focus on anything until it's been recorded or written down," she told NYU students in her 2022 commencement speech.

The path a song takes is different every time. Sometimes the whole song comes spilling out in one giant gush. Other times, a concept can take years. "We Are Never Getting Back Together" and "Tim McGraw" each took less than a half hour to complete; "All Too Well," on the other hand, took years.

The songwriting process is ephemeral, hard to explain. To hear Taylor tell it, it's a lot like magic. "I've never really been able to fully explain songwriting other than it's like this little glittery cloud floats in front

HITSTORY: "All Too Well"

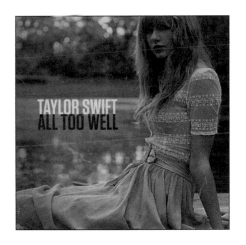

It can feel awful at the time, but sometimes the best art comes from heartbreak. "It was a day [in 2012] when I was just, like, a broken human, walking into rehearsal, just feeling terrible about what was going on in my personal life," Taylor said in a *Rolling Stone* podcast in 2020. "I just started playing four chords over and over again, and the band started kicking in. People just started playing along with me; I think they could tell I was really going through it. I just started singing and riffing and ad-libbing this song that basically was [*Red*'s] 'All Too Well.'" A longtime fan favorite, the 10-minute expanded version featured on *Red (Taylor's Version)* hit No. 1 on the Billboard charts in 2022, 10 years after its initial release. Though she has never explicitly confirmed who it was written about, it's a breakup anthem for the ages.

NILS SJÖBERG

Who is the mysterious Swede who struck gold as the writer of the 2016 Calvin Harris/ Rihanna megahit "This Is What You Came For"? For years there was speculation among Swifties that it was none other than Taylor herself. She was dating Calvin Harris at the time he produced the track, they reasoned. And it sounds like a Taylor Swift song…doesn't it? Taylor proved the internet sleuths right in 2020, when she revealed her hand in the creation in an interview with *Rolling Stone*. Like so many times before, she recorded a voice memo of herself working out a tune on the piano. She sent it to Harris; they both agreed it was a hit. But that wasn't the first time Sjöberg was credited as a songwriter. Taylor has used her nom de plume to write for artists including Sugarland, Little Big Town, B.o.B., Boys Like Girls, and even the fictional Hannah Montana. "I think when a pseudonym comes in is when you still have a love for making the work, and you don't want the work to become overshadowed by…what people know about you," she told *Rolling Stone*. And speaking of pseudonyms, check Taylor's own liner notes. William Bowery, a cowriter on both *Folklore* and *Evermore*, is none other than boyfriend Joe Alwyn.

of your face, and you grab it at the right time. And then you revert back to what you know about the structure of a song in order to fill in the gaps," she told the *New York Times.*

As a creator, she sees the world with eyes wide-open to inspiration. She wrote "Ronan" after reading a mother's essay about her son having cancer. "Tolerate It"

was inspired by the gothic novel *Rebecca* by Daphne du Maurier. A bibliophile, Taylor often finds sparks for song ideas in literature: allusions to Shakespeare ("Love Story"), Dickens ("Getaway Car"), Charlotte Brontë ("Invisible Strings"), and many others have made their way into her lyrics.

Of course, as an artist she's best known for writing about her own life experiences. "Music is my way of understanding what I'm feeling. It's carried me my whole life and allowed me to filter through complicated emotions and make them simple," she told *Songwriter Universe*.

Taylor has said that music is not only a way to process her own feelings, but it gives her a forum to say what she wants to say in the most elegant and straightforward way. "The reason why I keep doing it is because it's like a message in a bottle," she told the *New York Times*.

"You can put this message in a bottle, throw it out into the ocean, and maybe someday, the person that you wrote that song about is going to hear it and understand exactly how you felt.... It's conveying a message to someone that's more real than what you had the courage to say in person."

Being honest in her songwriting is a virtue that her fans cherish, but it's also been a nuisance. For a while, it seemed like the media was more interested in which ex she'd written a song about than they were the music itself. Over the years, frustrations over being seen chiefly as an artist who mines her own relationships for song fodder spurred her to stretch herself even further. She wrote clapback songs like "Blank Space"

> "Creativity is getting inspiration and having that lightning-bolt idea moment and then having the hard-work ethic to sit down at the desk and write it down."
>
> —TAYLOR TO *VOGUE*

and "Vigilante Shit" as direct responses to such criticisms. But it also led her to create more novelistic albums in *Folklore* and *Evermore*, both of which she penned during the COVID-19 pandemic.

Taylor has worked with countless producers, cowriters, and engineers during the creative process over her career. Like any artist, she has a particular rapport with certain collaborators: early on with cowriting cohort Liz Rose, and more recently with producer and the National front man Aaron Dessner, with whom she worked on recent albums *Folklore* and *Evermore*, and Jack Antonoff, who has producing credit on her last five studio albums, starting with *1989* in 2014. "[Jack's] excitement and exuberance about writing songs is contagious," Taylor told the *New York Times* in 2017. "He's an

Taylor often sits at the piano to work out ideas in developing songs.

absolute joy. That's why everyone loves him. I personally wouldn't trust someone who didn't."

Antonoff, best known for performing in bands including fun. and Bleachers, credits Taylor with opening the door to his producing career. "I'd been trying to produce for a while, but there was always some industry herb going, 'That's cute, but that's not your lane,'" he told the *New Yorker* in 2022. "Taylor was the first person with the stature to go, 'I like the way this sounds, I'm putting it on my album'—and then, suddenly, I was allowed to be a producer." (As of this writing, Antonoff has won two Producer of the Year Grammys for his work.) There's no denying he and Taylor make beautiful music together.

Ten albums—including two full-length offerings during the pandemic—prove what everyone not living under a rock already knows: Taylor was born to make music. It's what drives her, what feeds her soul, and ultimately what brings her the most joy.

"There's a common misconception that artists have to be miserable in order to make good art, that art and suffering go hand in hand," she reflected to the *New York Times* in 2022. "I'm really grateful to have learned this isn't true." •

Chapter Three
THE MASTERMIND

Suited up at the Sundance Film Festival for the premiere of *Miss Americana* in 2020.

Forget girlboss; Taylor Swift is just a boss, period. She's one of the most successful recording artists of all time. Her last eight albums have debuted at No. 1, most of them eclipsing a million copies sold in their first week. Her latest, *Midnights*, was the highest yet, selling 1.578 million units in its debut week, the biggest album release since Adele's *25* in 2015, reported Billboard. According to Bloomberg, that earned label Universal a tidy $230 million.

Four years earlier, in 2018, Swift ditched her former label, Big Machine, after a protracted fight to buy rights to the masters of her recordings ended with the label selling them out from under her. "For years, I asked, pleaded for a chance to own my work," she wrote on social media. "Instead I was given an opportunity to sign back up to Big Machine Records and 'earn' one album back at a time, one for every new one I turned in. I walked away because I knew once I signed that contract, Scott Borchetta would sell the label, thereby selling me and my future. I had to make the excruciating choice to leave behind my past."

$570
million

Taylor's net worth in 2022, according to *Forbes*.

Borchetta did sell the label, and Taylor's catalog of work along with it, for $300 million in 2019. Taylor signed a new deal with Universal, in which she retained the ownership of her masters, beginning with *Lover*. With her past work suddenly in the hands of a private investor, notorious uber-manager Scooter Braun, Taylor was distraught. "Let me just say that the definition of toxic male privilege in our industry is people saying 'But he's always been nice to me' when I'm raising valid concerns about artists and their rights to own their music. And of course he's nice to you; if you're in this room, you have something he needs," she said at Billboard's Women in Music event in 2019. "The fact is that private equity is what enabled this man to think, according to his own social media posts, that he could 'buy me.' But I'm obviously not going willingly."

She didn't just get mad, she got even, making the decision to re-record her music. "I just figured I was the one who made this music first; I can just make it again," she told *Late Night with Seth Meyers*.

Fearless (Taylor's Version) and *Red (Taylor's Version)* were released in 2021, both debuting at No. 1 on the Billboard charts. What's more, because of her clout in the industry, she was able to convince America's top radio network, iHeartRadio, to ditch the old recordings and play her newly recorded versions instead. Plans for new versions of *Taylor Swift*, *Speak Now*, and *Reputation* are in the offing as well.

"Taylor Swift is an economic genius," said Alan Krueger, former chairman of the Council of Economic Advisers under Obama and author of *Rockonomics*. The book explains the shift in the music industry. Years ago, record sales were the primary income for musicians. But as labels gobbled up more and more of that revenue share for themselves, touring became the primary moneymaker for artists.

Perhaps no one has harnessed the power of touring quite like Taylor. Her record-breaking Reputation tour made that crystal-clear, and she's poised to have an even bigger return with the 2023 Eras tour.

Taylor plays to a sold-out crowd of more than 53,000 at Cowboys Stadium on a 2013 tour stop in Arlington, Texas.

As the recent chaos with Ticketmaster made evident, Swifties' demand for concert tickets is unrivaled. (More on this later.)

Considering most of a musical artist's income is derived from concert revenue, which includes ticket sales and merchandise, it's staggering to learn that without a single performance, Taylor still landed at No. 25 on Forbes's list of Highest-Paid Entertainers in 2022. She's also one of the highest overachievers on the magazine's 2022 Richest Self-Made Women Under 40 list.

Taylor has also made a great deal of money by doing commercial endorsements. She's a pitchwoman in demand, who's inked deals with giant brands including Starbucks, Peloton, Apple, UPS, and Coca-Cola. She has a promotional deal with Target, selling a special edition of all her albums with the retailer that offers bonus content fans can't get anywhere else.

HITSTORY: "The Man"

"The Man" is a veritable poke in the eye of the patriarchy. Taylor describes the song as a thought experiment, wondering how the media would have described her career and treated her were she male. "If I had made all the same choices, all the same mistakes, all the same accomplishments, how would it read?" she posited to *Vogue*. "They'd say I hustled, put in the work. / They wouldn't shake their heads and question how much of this I deserve. / What I was wearing, if I was rude, / Could all be separated from my good ideas and power moves," goes the verse. It's a fair point, but the song is also a bop. "I wanted to make it catchy for a reason," Taylor told *Billboard* upon its release. "So that it would get stuck in people's heads, [so] they would end up with a song about gender inequality stuck in their heads. And for me, that's a good day."

Vamping with fellow COVERGIRLS (L to R) Ellen DeGeneres, Drew Barrymore, Dania Ramirez, and Queen Latifah.

Rocking Keds at a 2015
promotional event in
New York.

Taylor's portfolio is impressive, to say the least. She has not one but two private jets. According to *Elle Decor*, she owns more than $80 million in real estate, including her seaside estate in Westerly, Rhode Island (where her epic Fourth of July parties were held); her 11,000-square-foot Beverly Hills mansion (that once belonged to producer Samuel Goldwyn, the *G* in MGM); her secluded home base in Nashville; and multiple properties in New York's Tribeca and West Village neighborhoods.

If she's been successful beyond her wildest dreams, it certainly isn't by luck. "No one is this good and works harder," said Jack Antonoff, her longtime collaborator and friend. Indeed, Taylor's work ethic is legendary.

An unabashed feminist, Taylor believes that women have to work many times harder than their male counterparts. "The female artists that I know of have reinvented themselves 20 times more than the male artists. They have to, or else you're out of a job," she said in *Miss Americana*. "Constantly having to reinvent, constantly finding new facets of yourself that people find to be shiny" is a double standard in an

> ## "Swift isn't just a great songwriter: She's an unparalleled marketing genius."
>
> ## —*FORTUNE*

industry that is already notorious for being predatory, according to Taylor.

Considering all this, it's little wonder that her post–Big Machine records address the dust-up with her formal label head-on, pointedly discussing it in songs such as *Folklore*'s "My Tears Ricochet" ("And when you can't sleep at night / You hear my stolen lullabies") and *Midnights*' "Vigilante Shit," as well as *Lover*'s "The Man," in which Taylor muses about how people would react to her career had she been a male rather than female artist.

But as time marches on, it's clear that she's no longer a female artist in a man's world. As none other than trailblazer Barbara Walters put it, "Taylor Swift *is* the music industry." •

Chapter Four
THE INNOVATOR

Ever the innovator, Taylor keeps her eyes firmly fixed on the future.

Taylor's musical education started early. Like so many others, it began with the influence of her parents. She loved arena rockers like Def Leppard, country queens such as Patsy Cline and Tammy Wynette, modern country stars like Shania Twain and Faith Hill, and singer-songwriters such as James Taylor and Carole King in equal measure.

There was particularly something in country music that especially resonated with her. "I think it was the storytelling that grabbed me," she told *Blender*. A born storyteller herself, unspooling a narrative has been the focus of her music since the very beginning. Through all her innovations, her storytelling remains the through line that ties all her music together.

Taylor is an artist who consistently defies expectations—an artist constantly reaching for something more, better, different. Changing lanes is a difficult gambit for a singer. Experiment too much and you risk losing fans. Don't change enough and you're accused of being one-note. But Taylor

> "I've learned that the difference between those who can continue to create in [a toxic] climate [and those who cannot] usually comes down to this: who lets that scrutiny break them and who just keeps making art."
>
> —TAYLOR, ACCEPTING WOMAN OF THE DECADE HONORS FROM BILLBOARD IN 2019

has walked that tightrope beautifully. Her knack for reinvention is masterful, and the breadth and depth of her own musical influences are ever-growing, which is a testament to her authenticity as an artist and her commitment to her own craft.

The intricacies of Taylor's music could fill volumes, but the following is an album-by-album rundown of her ever-evolving musical style, in 10 quick hits.

Releasing her first record as a teenager, Taylor's debut album, *Taylor Swift*, spooled out almost like the pages of her diary. Listeners heard firsthand the heartache and hopefulness that peppered her young life. Two of that album's gems portray opposite sides of the breakup coin with deft precision. While "Tim McGraw" is a bittersweet sendoff to a lost relationship, "Picture to Burn" is more of a fired-up get-lost anthem. The album made her an instant darling in the country music world.

She continued to showcase her songwriting chops on *Fearless*. It became a breakout album with pop crossover hits such as "Love Story" and "You Belong with Me." Suddenly everyone knew the girl with the curly blonde hair, cowboy boots, and glittery guitar. Critics were taking notice too; she also won four Grammys for the effort, including Album of the Year.

Speak Now pushed Taylor's limits even further. Working without a cowriter for the first time, she owns full songwriting credits on the record. She also put her efforts into strengthening her vocals, bolstering those romantic ballads and pop anthems alike.

Red, Taylor's emotionally wrought fifth album, delivered another version of

heartbreak in all its messy glory, perhaps more vividly than ever before. This time, however unfair, the tabloids ripped her for it.

The backlash spurred her to move in a completely different direction, recording *1989*. A genuine pop album, there is not a trace of country on it. It is filled with countless hits, including tracks such as "Shake It Off" and "Blank Space," in which she thumbs her nose at the haters. She spoke in 2019 about how all the criticism spurred her to keep stretching herself—to prove people wrong: "I decided I would be what they said I couldn't be."

HITSTORY: "Lover"

Like many of Swift's songs, this one came to her like a bolt from the blue. She sprang from bed in the middle of the night to record the chorus stuck in her head, nearly identical to what features on the finished track. Talking to the *New York Times*, she explained the vibe of the song to a *T*: "I've been thinking for years that it would be great to have a song that people in love would want to…slow dance to. In my head I had just the last two people on the dance floor at 3 AM, swaying." The spare instrumentation and muted percussion give just the right flavor, befitting a couple that feels like they're the only two people in the world.

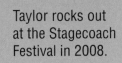

Taylor rocks out at the Stagecoach Festival in 2008.

Reputation took that pushback a step further. It was a declaration of independence: she was freeing herself from the shackles of toxic criticism for good. Becoming the caricature the media painted her to be, this record is full of edge, defiance, and a healthy dose of revenge.

Gone was the romantic, frilly Taylor of old; this version of Taylor was brash, bold, and unwilling to back down from a fight.

The *Reputation* statement safely made, *Lover* moved the goal posts once more. Songs range from the intimate, sultry title track to the ebullient "You Need to

PEN PALS

Accepting honors for Songwriter-Artist of the Decade at the Nashville Songwriter Awards in 2022, Taylor perfectly described how her writing style falls into three distinct categories. She explained that there are three types of songs and three metaphorical "pens" with which she writes them.

The first type of song, a **fountain pen** song, paints "a vivid picture of a situation, down to the chipped paint on the doorframe and the incense dust on the vinyl shelf." Drilling down into the details to color in the lines of a story is a common practice for Taylor, and you can hear it reflected in songs from "Our Song" to "All Too Well" to "Lavender Haze."

The second type is the **quill pen** song, such as the Shakespearean "Love Story," in which "the words and phrasings are antiquated," like "a letter written by Emily Dickinson's great-grandmother while sewing a lace curtain."

Then there's the brilliantly termed **glitter gel pen** song, pop confections such as "Shake It Off": "Frivolous, carefree, bouncy, syncopated perfectly to the beat. Glitter gel pen lyrics don't care if you don't take them seriously, because they don't take themselves seriously.… It's what we need every once in a while in these fraught times in which we live."

Performing at the 2019 American Music Awards, Taylor sheds the metaphorical straitjacket of her previous albums.

Taylor greets fans at the 2022 MTV Video Music Awards.

Calm Down," a sly takedown of bigots. Taylor described the album to *Vogue* as "a love letter to love, in all of its maddening, passionate, exciting, enchanting, horrific, tragic, wonderful glory."

In 2020, free from the commitments of touring, the pandemic brought a bounty of music to Swifties. First came *Folklore*, which was produced remotely by longtime producer Jack Antonoff and new collaborator Aaron Dessner. Musically, the folk-tinged record was new territory; it was also a departure lyrically, a concept album telling the story of three fictional teenagers caught in a love triangle. She made clear to followers upon its release that this was not a typical Taylor album, writing, "In isolation my imagination has run wild and this album is the result, a collection of songs and stories that flowed like a stream of consciousness. Picking up a pen was my way of escaping into fantasy, history, and memory. I've told these stories to the best of my ability with all the love, wonder, and whimsy they deserve. Now it's up to you to pass them down."

Then came *Evermore*—the "sister record" to *Folklore*—just five months later. Swift wrote, "To put it plainly, we just couldn't stop writing songs. To try and put it more poetically, it feels like we were standing on the edge of the folklorian woods and had a choice: to turn and go back or to travel further into the forest of this music. We chose to wander deeper in." *Spin* proclaimed it "the best work of her career," writing that with each album "she ascends further into the pantheon of songwriters who consistently deliver despite unimaginable expectations."

Flash forward to the present day, and the consensus is clear: she's done it once again. As *PopMatters* wrote in its 2022 review of *Midnights*, "It allows Swift to do what she has always wanted: make an album for its own sake that is received primarily as a work of art instead of a commercial entity or tabloid fodder. Indeed, on *Midnights* she is more self-assured than ever—letting more go, taking more chances, and making no apologies." Taylor describes it as a concept album, a creative exercise pondering what keeps people up at night.

When you put it all together, these albums comprise an incredible outpouring of work. But at just 33 years old, Taylor undoubtedly has so much ahead of her. Given her capacity for innovation, where she will go next is really anyone's guess. •

CRITICAL MASS

Since Taylor's debut with *Taylor Swift* in 2006, music critics have sung her praises. Following is a small sampling.

"Taylor wrote or cowrote everything on **TAYLOR SWIFT** herself (including the hit 'Tim McGraw'), and while the most immediately striking songs are her eviscerations of no-good teenage boys ('Should've Said No,' 'Picture to Burn'), the more thoughtful material suggests a talent poised to last well past high school," predicted *Country Weekly.* Even the grumps at *Pitchfork* called Taylor's debut "a solid, spunky-yet-reflective country record told squarely from the teenage perspective."

James Reed of the *Boston Globe* raved, "She's 18—wide-eyed, naive, hopeful—and that's how she sounds on **FEARLESS**, her superb new album." *L* magazine's Tom Breihan concurred, writing, "There might be someone out there making better pop music right now, but I sure haven't heard her."

Awarding the album four out of four stars, *Rolling Stone* wrote, "Swift's third album…is roughly twice as good as 2008's *Fearless*, which was roughly twice as good as her 2006 debut." Writing in *Stereogum* in 2020, James Rettig describes a Taylor teetering between being a teenager and an adult: "**SPEAK NOW** perfectly captures the imperfect moment when you're letting go of your old self to become someone new. It's sad having to grow up so fast, but it's inevitable."

"Lyrically, it's…deeper and a little darker…. Musically, it's bigger and bolder than anything she's ever done in the pop world," wrote *Entertainment Weekly*, awarding it a B+. *Slant* magazine presciently wrote that **RED** boasts "career-best work for Swift, who now sounds like the pop star she was destined to be all along."

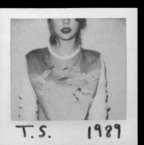

Heralding Taylor's departure from country music for pop, the *New York Times* wrote of **1989**, "By making pop with almost no contemporary references, Ms. Swift is aiming somewhere even higher, a mode of timelessness that few true pop stars…even bother aspiring to. Everyone else striving to sound like now will have to shift gears once the now sound changes. But not Ms. Swift, who's waging, and winning, a new war, one she'd never admit to fighting."

The *Los Angeles Times* heralded **REPUTATION** as "her most focused, most cohesive album to date," and the *Guardian* called it "a master class of pop songwriting." Wrote *Spin* in its rave, "Never has she sounded freer than she does here, a self-styled villain biting the forbidden fruit of gossip and letting its juices run down her neck."

"As always, **LOVER** is an album Swift made for her fans. But it also feels like a record she made for herself, unburdened by external expectations and her own past," wrote the *A.V. Club*. *Variety* described it as "[an] exuberant album…. Event Pop where the sharing of emotions on a massive scale is the richest part of the blockbuster occasion."

Rolling Stone described **FOLKLORE** as a surprise album full of, well, surprises: "The most head-spinning, heartbreaking, emotionally ambitious songs of her life." *Paste* magazine called it "one of her best, most perfectly produced projects ever. In *Folklore*, she wrote a quieter, more thought-provoking chapter in her constantly shape-shifting story."

In its five-star review of **EVERMORE**, *NME* wrote, "If *Folklore* is an introspective, romantic older sister, *Evermore* is the freewheeling younger sibling. *Folklore* was Swift's masterful songwriting spun through a very specific sonic palette; *Evermore* feels looser, with more experimentation, charm and musical shades at play. The new album reaps the rewards of the stylistic leap of faith that *Folklore* represented, pushing the boundaries of that sonic palette further still."

Examining Taylor's latest, NPR declared, "Accessing the vibes projected by the TikTok confessionalists who are her spiritual children and the genre-agnostic singer-songwriters reconfiguring indie pop and R&B as she once did in country, Swift uses **MIDNIGHTS** as a way to rethink the sonic rhetoric of first-person storytelling and shake off habits that have served her artistically and commercially for more than a decade."

Chapter Five
THE PERFORMER

Taylor and Karyn
take the stage on
the Reputation tour.

There's nothing quite like a Taylor Swift concert. Just ask one of the millions of fans who have seen her perform live since she first became a touring artist.

Taylor became the most successful touring artist in history when her Reputation tour smashed the record for the highest-grossing US tour of all time, earning $345 million after only 38 dates. (And by the way, that eye-popping figure doesn't include earnings from the deal with Netflix, granting the streamer exclusive filming rights on the tour, and the resultant concert film.)

Why was it such a blockbuster success? For one thing, she puts on a show with a capital *S*. A lifelong fan of Broadway musicals, she knows how to stage a grand spectacle, including huge set pieces, droves of dancers, and a robust supporting cast of musicians. For the Reputation tour, she embraced a snake theme full-on, turning Kim Kardashian's invective about her into a positive. (Kardashian weighed in on the controversy surrounding the lyrics in her then-husband Kanye West's song "Famous," which

denigrated Swift. Swift claims that she was blindsided, but Kardashian demurred, infamously calling Swift a snake to her millions of followers on social media.)

"I learned that disarming someone's petty bullying can be as simple as learning to laugh," Swift wrote in *Elle*. "I can't tell you how hard I had to keep from laughing every time my 63-foot inflatable cobra named Karyn appeared onstage in front of 60,000 screaming fans."

$9
million

According to *Business Insider*, Taylor earned an estimated $9 million per concert on her Reputation tour.

That Taylor has been able to achieve such ardent in-person support through concert attendance is a testament to the unique connection she has with her fan base. She plays all the way to the rafters, but she also reaches for quieter moments of intimacy. "The challenge with a stadium show is making those people in the very top row feel like they got an intimate, personal experience," she told *Time*. "On the Red tour we achieved that sense of intimacy by having acoustic moments, and moments where I was telling stories about these songs. I don't like to scream at the audience, I like to talk to them." It's an ethos she brings to all of her stadium shows, punctuating the bigger moments with quieter ones.

The specifics of each new tour become known to fans as soon as Taylor hits the road, but she still tries to incorporate the element of surprise whenever possible, swapping out which songs she plays during acoustic breaks and bringing in surprise guests in each new city. She also takes fan feedback from social media into account when choosing acoustic songs, and plays covers from the native sons and daughters of the city in which she's playing. (For instance, she did a mash-up of Bruce Springsteen and Bon Jovi on concert stops in New Jersey.)

Taylor hasn't been on tour since 2018's Reputation tour. (Her planned Lover Fest tour, in support of *Lover*, was scuttled by the pandemic in 2020.) Given that, when her 2023 Eras tour was first announced—billed by Taylor as "a journey through the musical eras of my career (past and present!)"—it was reasonable to expect there'd be excitement. What most people didn't expect, however, was that it would break the internet.

Demand for presale tickets was so high that Ticketmaster's website

In Newark, New Jersey, on the Speak Now world tour in 2011.

MUST-SEE T.S.

Taylor's onstage prowess is legendary. If you haven't had the opportunity to see her perform live in person, pop over to YouTube and check out these 10 killer performances.

10. Belting out the *Red* track "I Knew You Were Trouble" on the 1989 World Tour—that high note!

9. Vamping "Style" on the runway alongside pal Karlie Kloss and other Victoria's Secret Angels at the Victoria's Secret Fashion Show in 2014.

8. The spectacle of "I Did Something Bad" on her Reputation tour.

7. Performing "Fifteen" with Miley Cyrus at the 2009 Grammy Awards, Taylor's first-ever stint on the Grammy stage.

6. Her rendition of "Blank Space" at the GRAMMY Museum in 2015—worth it for the introduction alone!

5. Performing the anthemic "Out of the Woods" from the 1989 tour.

4. The fairy-tale-tinged *Folklore/Evermore* medley of "Cardigan," "August," and "Willow" at the 2021 Grammys.

3. Her delicate rendition of "Holy Ground" on the piano at the BBC Radio 1's Live Lounge in 2019.

2. The epic medley of "The Man," "Love Story," "I Knew You Were Trouble," "Blank Space," and "Shake It Off," featuring a little help from her friends Camila Cabello and Halsey, while celebrating her Artist of the Decade honors at the 2019 American Music Awards.

1. "All Too Well" (10-minute version) on the November 13, 2021, episode of *Saturday Night Live*, alongside her short film of the same name.

Performing at the
2013 BRIT Awards.

Having fun Down Under
performing on the 1989 World
Tour in Melbourne, Australia.

completely shut down due to unprecedented traffic, leaving devastated Swifties out in the cold. Pre-verified ticket buyers waited hours in virtual waiting rooms for their guaranteed tickets before being told they were out of luck. What's more, the vendor announced that general sales for Eras were canceled due to lack of inventory. The fiasco made national headlines and took weeks to sort out. It even drew the ire of lawmakers, who railed against the ticket broker's monopoly. "Ticketmaster—I knew you were trouble way back in 2009 when I asked questions about your ticketing practices as AG. Long story short, your anti-competitive behavior has been no love story for Taylor Swift concertgoers," tweeted Connecticut senator Richard Blumenthal. Swift apologized to fans, calling the disaster "excruciating." She also added more tour dates, extending Eras from 27 shows to 52, to accommodate the demand.

For those lucky enough to have scored a ticket, Eras promises to be a return to form for the artist, whose onstage prowess is unrivaled. The US leg will span 20 US cities, with multiple performances in each location. Not many artists can sell out a

HIT STORY: "Look What You Made Me Do"

Sometimes revenge can be sweet indeed. Taylor's first single off her 2017 album *Reputation* is a banger onstage. It sets fire to her tabloid image— "I'm sorry, the old Taylor can't come to the phone right now / Why? Oh, 'cause she's dead," she deadpans. She also takes down some of her most high-profile adversaries, portrayed pointedly in the accompanying music video, including sleazy disc jockeys, greedy streaming companies, bitter exes, and the VMA-crasher-in-chief himself, Kanye West.

Chapter Five
THE PERFORMER

Taylor performs for fans in Los Angeles on August 21, 2015, during the 1989 World Tour.

stadium to begin with; Taylor is selling out in Los Angeles's SoFi Stadium *five* nights. She'll be supported by female-fronted and queer acts including Haim, Paramore, Phoebe Bridgers, girl in red, Gracie Abrams, Muna, beabadoobee, and Gayle, as well as former backup dancer–turned-singer and "Lover" music video costar Owenn.

"I can't WAIT to see your gorgeous faces out there," Swift wrote on Instagram in 2022. "It's been a long time coming."

On the Eras tour, fans can surely expect to hear some of Taylor's new-old songs from her recorded albums *Red (Taylor's Version)* and *Fearless (Taylor's Version)*—including that epic 10-minute "All Too Well," no doubt—in addition to a healthy dose of tracks from her recent albums, including *Midnights, Evermore,* and *Folklore.* But the surest bet will be to expect the unexpected.

After a long hiatus away from touring, Taylor's ready to get on the road again and affirm the bonds she has with her fan base. "The most potent way that you can see [fans] react is when you're looking in their faces.... I miss that connection," she told *The Tonight Show Starring Jimmy Fallon* in 2022. ●

Chapter Six
THE BESTIE

With Abigail Anderson at the 2015 Grammy Awards.

There is a certain girl-next-door quality to Taylor. Something relatable, something accessible. Something in her music that resonates so deeply and is so *right on* that it feels like she can't be talking to anyone but you.

Certainly Taylor is a skilled poet of the human experience. She writes about all the messy feelings and mistakes and triumphs that people endure universally. So it's little surprise that she's been described as America's best friend. As many Swifties would attest, "She gets us!"

Indeed, she is well-known for her many famous friends—everyone from Ed Sheeran to Emma Stone to Ina Garten. Her legendary Fourth of July parties, thrown for years at her beach house in Rhode Island until 2016, were reliably a who's who of A-listers that would make any paparazzo drool.

When asked in 2014 by *Good Morning America* about her many friendships across the entertainment industry, she commented, "I think that it doesn't matter what career my friends have. It's just based on the fact that I can really relate to people who are driven and intelligent. You want to be around, like, smart, exciting people. I think that's what brings you up."

To be asked to defend why you have so many friendships is silly to begin with, but Taylor takes it all in stride. If there's one thing she knows how to do, it's deflect criticism. "There are a lot of really easy ways to dispel rumors. If they say you have fake friendships, all you have to do is continue to be there for each other," she told *Vogue*.

Taylor says that her spirit animal is a dolphin because they're very social and travel in groups.

To a person, Taylor's friends describe her as a loyal, kind, and generous pal. She's the kind who goes out of her way to offer support and be their champion. Selena Gomez, who met Taylor back in 2008 when they were dating brothers Nick and Joe Jonas, respectively, is one of Taylor's biggest champions. "The reason why [Swift's] one of my best friends is because this person has never, ever judged me for a decision I've made. She's always met me where I've been," Gomez said onstage

> "You sit in class next to a redhead named Abigail / And soon enough you're best friends."
>
> —FROM "FIFTEEN"

"I am such a girls' girl.... I love people who have a sense of ambition and passion for what they do but are also spontaneous and fun and can make you laugh when you have a hard day." —To *AM Tonight*

during a performance with Taylor in 2018. "She encouraged me when I had nothing to be encouraged about. And I don't know if I would be as strong as I am if I didn't have [her and her] family."

"Taylor has always been so kind and supportive and also goes out of her way to give young artists advice," Camila Cabello told *Bustle* in 2021. "She's really about making friendships and relationships the most important thing."

"She's amazing for being a champion, and making things better for the generations to come," Jack Antonoff told *NME* in 2021.

Actress Blake Lively and Taylor have been close since meeting in 2015, and are staunch supporters of one another in their careers and lives. "Aunt Taylor" even gave the characters central to her *Folklore* album the names of Lively and Ryan Reynolds's children: James, Betty, and Inez. (Audio of a young James also appears on Taylor's song "Gorgeous.")

Taylor is also still tight with her BFF from Hendersonville, Abigail Anderson,

---

HITSTORY: "Shake It Off"

It's like I got this music in my mind sayin' its gonna be alright.

The entire *1989* album is a celebration of the joys of female friendship, but no track is more anthemic than "Shake It Off," which forever belongs on every girls' night playlist. Cowritten with pop maestro Max Martin and Shellback, the lyrics read like they're from the pages of a BFF's playbook, reminding you that no one has the power to make you feel anything without your consent. "These are things that we go through in every phase of our life...[when] there's just someone who has it out for you," Taylor said to *AM Tonight* in 2014. So let the haters hate and the players play, and in the immortal words of Taylor, shake it off!

THE TAO OF TAYLOR

Sometimes it feels like Taylor could be your bestie. Her lyrics tap into your experiences and make you feel like she knows *exactly* what you're going through. So next time you ask yourself, *What would Taylor do?,* consider some of her best BFF-worthy advice, below.

"Grow a backbone, trust your gut, and know when to strike back. Be like a snake: only bite if someone steps on you." —To *Elle*

"No matter what love throws at you, you have to believe in it. You have to believe in love stories and Prince Charmings and happily ever after." —From the liner notes to *Fearless*

"[Live] your life based on what your grandkids will say one day." —To *Time*

"You shouldn't care so much if you feel misunderstood by a lot of people who don't know you, as long as you feel understood by the people who do know you, the people who will show up for you, the people who see you as a human being." —Onstage in 2018

"One thing about learning to be the best friend you can possibly be is knowing when to let people figure out things on their own." —To 2DayFM radio, Sydney, Australia

"Enthusiasm can protect you from anything. You can come back, even if you have a failure, you're rejected or criticized for something, you can become enthusiastic about the next thing." —To BBC Radio 1

"Real love doesn't mess with your head. Real love just is. Real love just endures. Real love maintains. Real love takes it page by page." —Taylor's maid of honor speech at friend Britany Maack's 2016 nuptials, as reported by *Vogue*

"The only real risk is being too afraid to take a risk at all." —To the *Wall Street Journal*

"When you say someone is canceled, it's not a TV show. It's a human being. You're sending mass amounts of messaging to this person to either shut up, disappear, or [worse]." —To *Vogue*

"I know it can be really overwhelming figuring out who to be, and when. Who you are now and how to act in order to get where you want to go. I have some good news: It's totally up to you. I also have some terrifying news: It's totally up to you." —From her 2022 NYU commencement speech

FRIENDS ARE FOREVER

Swifties know Taylor is big into *Dateline*, and she named her cats after characters from *Grey's Anatomy* and *Law & Order: SVU*, but her heart forever belongs to the ride-or-die pals of *Friends*, which she often calls her favorite TV show.

whom she met when she was just 15. Swifties know that Abigail has appeared in many of her videos, including "Picture to Burn," "I'm Only Me When I'm with You," and "New Romantics," among others.

Of course, no discussion of Taylor's expert-level friendship would be complete without mentioning her furry friends. Her two adorable Scottish fold cats Olivia Benson and Meredith Grey, and ragdoll cat Benjamin Button, feature prominently in her social media posts, music videos, and TV commercials. (And who says friendship doesn't have its privileges? According to Cats.com, Olivia is the third-richest pet in the world at $97 million because of her onscreen meow-ments.)

And through it all, no one has been steadier than Taylor's family—father Scott, brother Austin (who playfully calls his sis Taffy), and especially mom Andrea. "She's one of my best friends. She's always, always around. She's the person in my life who will...look me in the eye and say, 'Look, snap out of it,'" Taylor once said. And isn't that what best friendship is all about? •

Taylor gives a hug to her mother, Andrea, onstage at the ACMs in 2015 while accepting the 50th Anniversary Milestone Award for youngest ACM Entertainer of the Year. She has often referred to her mom as her best friend.

Chapter Seven
THE ADVOCATE

Women supporting women. Taylor stans Rachel Platten and her hit "Fight Song." The song was also Hillary Clinton's 2016 presidential campaign anthem.

In the music industry, it's hard to imagine a bigger advocate for other artists than Taylor Swift. Given her influence, she's been able to press for industry-wide change in a way that most other artists could not.

When the digital age upended the music business, with artists getting paid fractions of pennies for their work behind opaque algorithms from streaming sites, Taylor wrote an op-ed in the *Wall Street Journal* that read in part, "Music is art, and art is important and rare. Important, rare things are valuable. Valuable things should be paid for. It's my opinion that music should not be free."

She pulled her entire catalog of music from Spotify, full stop. "I'm not willing to contribute my life's work to an experiment that I don't feel fairly compensates the writers, producers, artists, and creators of this music," she told Yahoo. The moves against unfair streaming practices have had some effect. Her parent company, Universal (one of three major US labels), now allows all of their artists to opt out of streaming in their albums' first two weeks, giving them a chance to earn more through physical album sales.

Taylor also uplifts artists in other ways, promoting them whenever and however she can. A voracious consumer of music, Taylor is an unabashed fan who has brought on scores of tourmates whom she genuinely admires, from Haim to Phoebe Bridgers to Camila Cabello. It's important to Taylor that she lifts up other women around her, describing her fellow artists as a sorority of sorts. "Other women who are killing it should motivate you, thrill you, challenge you, and inspire you," she said to *Time* in 2014. But it's not just the ladies; Taylor brought the likes of Ed Sheeran, Shawn Mendes, and Vance Joy, among others, on the road when all three of their careers were in their infancy.

She's always been a staunch self-advocate, railing against sexism in the industry and standing firm when it counted. Songs such as "The Man" and "Miss Americana & the Heartbreak Prince" deal with the double standard pointedly,

65,000

Pundits called it the Taylor Swift Effect. Just 24 hours after posting on social media in support of Democratic candidates and the Equality Act—her very first public political statement—Vote.org reported a massive spike in new voter registrations, with more than 65,000 registrants in a single day.

but it's woven into the fabric of all of her music. She's also been quick to call out journalists more interested in her love life than her music, or who ask when she's going to have children or which ex her song is about. "People...say, 'Oh, you know, like, she just writes songs about her ex-boyfriends.' And I think frankly that's a very sexist angle to take. No one says that about Ed Sheeran. No one says that about Bruno Mars. They're all writing songs about their exes, their current girlfriends, their love life, and no one raises the red flag there," she told 2DayFM.

She's on a quest to dismantle the idea that *feminism* is a dirty word. "Misogyny is ingrained in people from the time they are born," Taylor told *Maxim* in December 2015. "So, to me, feminism is probably the most important movement that you could embrace, because it's just basically another word for equality. A man writing about his feelings from a vulnerable place is brave; a woman writing about her feelings from a vulnerable place is oversharing or whining."

Through the years, Taylor has taken more than her fair share of lumps from a media looking to criticize her. "I saw that

HITSTORY: "You Need to Calm Down"

If "Blank Space" was mud in the eye of haters, then "You Need to Calm Down" was the kill shot. While the song sounds like a bouncy pop tune, it's actually deadly serious. She lampoons keyboard warriors and anti-LGBTQ protestors with surgical precision. The final verse takes aim at misogynists who pit women against other women. The star-studded

video features LGBTQ icons including Ellen DeGeneres, Adam Lambert, RuPaul, and members of the *Queer Eye* cast. Taylor also appears alongside Katy Perry, dressed as a hamburger and fries, publicly burying their so-called "feud." Perry tweeted a still from the video to her followers, declaring it "BEEF-free."

With pal Todrick Hall at a performance of *Kinky Boots* on Broadway in 2016. Hall played Lola in the production.

people love to explain away a woman's success in the industry, and I saw something change in me due to this realization.... I became a mirror for my detractors. Whatever they decided I couldn't do is exactly what I did," she said in 2019. After winning a Grammy for Album of the Year for *Fearless*, critics said she didn't really write her own songs. She went out and made *Speak Now* without a single cowriter. When detractors accused her of dating too much, she stopped dating completely. "For years." When they said she wasn't country enough, she turned around and did a pure pop album.

It can't be denied that Taylor wears her emotions on her sleeve, never shying away from baring her soul through her music. But when it comes to speaking her mind about her political beliefs, it's been more of an uphill battle. The country music establishment was always quick to remind her of the Dixie Chicks, who were driven out of the industry after making an unflattering remark about then-president George W. Bush. "Part of the fabric of being a country artist is 'Don't force your politics on people.'... That is grilled into us," she said in *Miss Americana*. The documentary depicts her struggle to stay silent on her political views in the face of intense pressure from her label, inner circle, and even members of her own family.

Performing "Me!" at iHeartRadio's Wango Tango in 2019.

Giving the commencement address to NYU's class of 2022 at Yankee Stadium.

TAYLORED ARGUMENTS

After years of "being polite at all costs" and keeping out of politics, Taylor decided enough was enough, using her considerable platform to advocate for causes she believes in. Here's a brief timeline.

March 2018: Taylor writes in support of gun-control measures and the March for Our Lives movement.

October 2018: Taylor announces her support for Democratic candidates in the 2018 midterm elections, denouncing the so-called GOP slate of hate.

June 2019: Taylor writes an open letter to Tennessee senator Lamar Alexander in support of the Equality Act.

August 2019: Taylor calls the Trump presidency "an autocracy" and uses her VMA speech to thank fans who signed her petition for the passage of the Equality Act.

January 2020: Miss Americana is released. The documentary includes a behind-the-scenes look at Taylor's decision to jump into the political arena, plus some choice words for then–Senate candidate Marsha Blackburn.

May 2020: Taylor replies to an incendiary tweet from then-president Donald Trump, writing, "we will vote you out."

May 2022: Taylor speaks out for gun control once more in the aftermath of shootings in Buffalo, New York, and Uvalde, Texas.

June 2022: Writing to her followers on social media, Taylor voices despair over the Supreme Court's decision to overturn *Roe v. Wade*, stripping women of the right to choose.

"I need to be on the right side of history," she argued. When she posted her first-ever political post, standing against Tennessee candidate Marsha Blackburn for her racist, homophobic, and misogynistic policies, it didn't halve her fan base, as her camp had predicted. Instead, it drove up voter registration considerably. Blackburn did win her race, but Taylor had made her point, and she was still standing.

She credits her friend Todrick Hall with giving her the push that she needed to speak out. He asked her what she would think if her child were gay, and she was floored that he didn't already know how she felt. "If he was thinking that, I can't imagine what my fans in the LGBTQ community might be thinking," she went on. "It was kind of devastating to realize that I hadn't been publicly clear about [my support of that community]."

"Who you love and how you identify shouldn't put you in danger, leave you vulnerable or hold you back in life," she tweeted pointedly. She publicly petitioned for the Equality Act, starting a petition on Change.org that netted more than 800,000 signatures, eight times more than required for it to make its way to Congress for consideration. "I didn't realize until recently that I could advocate for a community that I'm not a part of," she told *Vogue*. The Equality Act, which provides protections against discrimination on the basis of sexual orientation and gender, was signed into law by President Joe Biden in 2022.

If promoting equal rights for everyone courts more controversy for Taylor, she's made peace with it. She's taken lumps before, and she's still standing. "Obviously anytime you're standing up for or against anything, you're never going to receive unanimous praise," she told *Variety* in 2020. "But that's what forces you to be brave. And that's what's different about the way I live my life now." •

> "I wanna love glitter and also stand up for the double standards that exist in our society. I wanna wear pink and tell you how I feel about politics, and I don't think that those things have to cancel each other out."
>
> —IN *MISS AMERICANA*

First Lady Michelle Obama presents Taylor with the Big Help Award, in recognition of Taylor's charity work, at the Nickelodeon Kids' Choice Awards in 2012.

...ift

Heartache &
...atinum Life

White
...ll Over
...rench Coats

THE
PEOPLE
ISSUE '09

BEST
DRI
&
OF

DR
YO
BE
5 W
TO
YOU
SHA

TIME

PO

TA
S

Rolling Stone

Issue 1216 September 25, 2014 $4.99

The
New
Life of
Taylor
Swift

FALL
PREVIEW

U2
Kendrick Lamar
Foo Fighters
Nicki Minaj
Stevie Nicks
Kanye West
Jackson Browne
Weezer
Charli XCX

CHINA
& GLOBAL
WARMING

The Fight
to Rein in
the World's
Biggest
Polluter

PLUS

ROBERT
PLANT
ANDRÉ
3000
BILL
HADER
APHEX
TWIN
NICK
CAVE

GLAMOUR

Taylor Swift

40
Little W
to Conn
With a G

YOU
BREAS

mujerhoy

GLA

750
Spring
Looks
For YOU

100
Best
Beauty
Tricks
Of 2014
Gorgeous
hair & skin
all year

112

Taylor
Swift

Pediatras

COSM

Oups!
MA PIRE
GAFFE
SEXUELLE

Au début
on était
amis...
Des amoureux
racontent

BONS PLANS
EXPÉRIENCES
ÉMOTIONS

Harper's

TAY
SW

Taylor greets fans in
Foxborough, Massachusetts,
on a 2018 tour stop.

Taylor has long maintained a serious connection with her fan base. She interacts with them regularly, communicating with her fans directly and often on her socials. "I'm always listening, and I'm always lurking. I'm always listening to their opinions and their theories," she told Seth Meyers in 2021. There's even a name for it: Swifties call it "Taylurking."

While that may sound sinister, what it really means is that Taylor is listening—listening to what her fans like (and don't) from her music. Listening to what songs they want to hear her play in concert. Listening about what's going on in their lives. She's described the connection with her fans as the longest and best relationship she's ever had, and it's one that she's invested in heavily over the years.

Examples are everywhere. She provides words of encouragement to fans going through difficult times and financial assistance to fans in need. She's even written songs about her fans. (*Red*'s "Ronan," for instance, was written for fan Maya Thompson, who lost her three-year-

old son to neuroblastoma; Taylor released the single in advance of the album and donated 100 percent of the proceeds to cancer research.)

At shows, she hosts marathon meet-and-greets where fans are encouraged to kick back and hang rather than rushed through a receiving line like most artists. "Fans are my favorite thing in the world," Taylor once said. "I've never been the type of artist who has that line drawn between their friends and their fans. The line's always been really blurred for me. I'll hang out with them after the show. I'll hang out with them before the show. If I see them in the mall, I'll stand there and talk to them for 10 minutes."

The fans are also among the very first people to hear her new music. Starting with *1989*, Taylor began staging secret listening parties (which became known as the Secret Sessions), previewing her new record several weeks in advance for some of her most ardent fans. "I had spent months picking fans on Instagram, Tumblr, Twitter—people who had been so supportive and had tried and tried to meet

92M

Watch out, Barack, the Swifties are coming! Taylor has built a massive following on Twitter, with 92 million followers and climbing, making her the ninth-most-followed account on the social media channel (trailing Obama's top mark of 133 million).

me, had been to five shows or however many events but had never met me before," she said to NPR in 2014. "And in every single one of my houses in the US and my hotel room in London, I would invite 89 people over to my living room, play them the entire album, tell them the stories behind it... We spent four hours together each night, taking Polaroids and having a great time and giving them a chance to tell me their stories that they wanted to tell in their own time. Not being rushed. Not having to feel panic. And then they went back out into the world." All the fans get sent home with a swag bag containing the unreleased album. Amazingly, or perhaps as a testament to Swifties' fidelity, nothing about the record was leaked in advance.

It was the fans who encouraged Taylor to release the original version of "All Too Well," which was cut from 10 minutes to 5 for the original *Red* release in 2012. And it was the fans who made "All Too Well (Taylor's Version)" the longest song ever to hit No. 1 on the Billboard charts.

Another way in which Taylor has been able to connect with her fans is through the Easter eggs she buries in her lyrics, music

HITSTORY: "Anti-Hero"

For a singer known for exploring her insecurities in song, "Anti-Hero" is next-level. Calling it among the favorite songs she's ever written, Taylor told followers on Instagram, "I don't think I've really delved this far into my insecurities in this detail before." It tackles head-on her struggles with anxiety and depression, isolation, and body image.

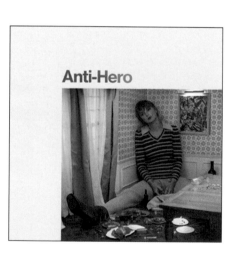

The video stirred major controversy when it depicted Swift stepping onto a scale that read *FAT*, causing the image to be redacted. (The star has recently been open about her struggles with eating disorders.) But while some felt triggered, most came to the artist's defense, applauding her candidness and relating to her vulnerabilities.

The scene in Times Square as fans turned out for a free *Good Morning America* concert in 2014.

Taylor held a 13-hour meet-and-greet for fans during the CMA Music Festival on June 13, 2010.

FAN CHAT

Taylor has found a variety of unique ways to connect with her fans, but at the end of the day, it's the music, more than anything, that reaches the masses. And it's in the music where fans connect most closely. It touches male and female, old and young, in equal measure. Here's just a small sampling.

"Taylor Swift's music is such a gift to the world, and the way she fosters community is so brilliant." —John Green, author of *The Fault in Our Stars*

"She has taught me that after a disappointment, you have to get back out there. Not for someone else, but for yourself." —Kate, age 10

"taylor swift being brave enough to use her platform to share and spread light on sensitive topics is one of the main reasons i will always love her." —@sntvalbum on Twitter

videos, and communications. Since her very first album, she's buried hidden messages in her liner notes, interspersing stray capital letters in her song lyrics. "When I was 15 and putting together my first album...I decided to encode the lyrics with hidden messages using capital letters," she told the *Washington Post*. "That's how it started, and my fans and I have since descended into color coding, numerology, word searches, elaborate hints, and Easter eggs."

The practice has turned Swifties into amateur cryptologists, speculating about songs' inspirations and spinning wild theories about music and what might be coming next. (Unsurprisingly, Taylor often chimes in to confirm or deny some of those theories.) Astute viewers and listeners are quick to point out the details buried in music videos, or oblique references woven into her lyrics.

"It's really about turning new music into an event for my fans and trying to entertain

THE INFLUENCER

them in playful, mischievous, clever ways," Taylor told the *Washington Post* in 2022. "As long as they still find it fun and exciting, I'll keep doing it."

Her direct interaction with her fans is certainly one of the reasons why she has a massive following on social media. As of this writing, she has more than 92 million followers on Twitter, 241 million on Instagram, 17 million on TikTok, 77 million on Facebook, and 51 million subscribers on YouTube. What's more, while some of social media's top dogs have seen relatively flat numbers over the past few years, her numbers keep climbing steadily.

Taylor was named the most influential person on Twitter by *Time* in 2018, despite only tweeting 13 times that year. And in 2019 she was named to Time's 100 Most Influential People list. Shawn Mendes, who wrote Swift's profile in the magazine, penned, "Taylor makes the job of creating music for millions of people look easy. It all comes from her—her belief in magic and love, and her ability to be as honest and raw as possible. She's the master of putting the perfect amount of thought into not overthinking, and that's why her music connects so well."

"All any...[artist] wants is to create something that will last, whatever it is in life.... All that matters to me is the memories that I've had with you," Taylor told fans when accepting the Artist of the Decade Award at the 2019 American Music Awards. "We've had fun, incredible, exhilarating, extraordinary times together." That alone is a legacy worth holding on to. ●

> "I want to make the most of this cultural relevance or success or whatever you want to call it, because it's not going to last. I have to be as good a person [as I can] while my name matters to them. Because it's not always going to matter to kids who are 15 and really struggling with who they want to be or [because] their friends were brutal to them at school that day. That's actual turmoil. I have to do everything I can to make their day better while I still can."
>
> —TAYLOR TO THE *TELEGRAPH* IN 2015

"I have the fans to thank, essentially, for my happiness," Taylor said in 2023.

Chapter Nine
THE FASHIONISTA

Sheer elegance at the
CMT Music Awards
in 2013.

Taylor has said that her biggest style icons are glamorous fashion titans and old Hollywood stars Grace Kelly and Audrey Hepburn. Both embodied an inarguable elegance and refinement that you can see imprinted in the DNA of Taylor's fashion sense. Never one to be too vulgar or sexy, Taylor has long opted for the prim, the sophisticated, and the classic.

She's also influenced by the unforgettable style of French chanteuse Françoise Hardy, the accomplished singer-songwriter and fashion iconoclast. Some of Taylor's best looks seem like they could be straight from the Hardy playbook: the striped tops and short shorts from the Red tour; the mirror-ball dresses she wore to the 2018 AMAs, the 2022 EMAs, and her surprise appearance at the 1975's London show in 2023; and the bohemian casualness of *Midnights* and the "Anti-Hero" video.

Fans like to categorize Taylor's style by eras—by the albums that were contemporaneous with her looks: The long, curly locks and diaphanous frocks of her debut (complete with cowboy boots,

8

The number of outfits Taylor wore onstage during each performance on the Reputation tour.

naturally). The glittery princess dresses of the *Fearless* era. The scarlet-soaked retro *Red* era. The off-duty model vibe of the *1989* years. The cottagecore whimsy of *Folklore* and *Evermore*.

To some degree these generalizations are accurate. "I can look back at an old photo and tell you roughly what year it's from," Swift told *Vogue* in 2016. "Going through different phases is one of my favorite things about fashion. I love how it can mark the passage of time. It's similar to my songs in that way—it all helps identify where I was at in different points of my life."

Her most dramatic style shift came when she moved to New York. The paparazzi were parked outside her door every day, waiting to get a salable shot of the star. She did not disappoint, turning the streets of New York, like many before her, into a real-life runway. That included lots of drool-worthy designer bags and her own signature spin on preppy perfection: knit beanies, peacoats, tights, and tweed, tweed, tweed.

Also, owing to her so-called squad of model friends, including Karlie Kloss, Gigi

Hadid, Cara Delevingne, Martha Hunt, and others, she incorporated many designer looks into her everyday wardrobe. It was definitely a style shift, with nary a cowboy boot in sight.

There is perhaps no higher stage for fashion than the Costume Institute Benefit, staged at New York's Metropolitan Museum of Art and known informally as the Met Gala. Taylor has been to six of them since she came onto the scene, giving her serious style cred. She attended her first in 2008. Befitting the ball's superhero theme, she was a glittering golden girl in a sequined slip dress by Badgley Mischka. In 2010 she wore iconic American designer Ralph Lauren to the Met's celebration of the American woman. The J. Mendel dress she wore to the "Alexander McQueen: Savage Beauty"–themed 2011 gala showed a style evolution; she was still romantic and demure, but there was a roughness to the layered gown. She wore J. Mendel again in 2013, a celebration of the punk

HITSTORY: "Cardigan"

cardigan + songwriting voice memo

While there are plenty of Taylor songs that celebrate her quirky sense of style, none have used fashion as a metaphor better than "Cardigan," off 2021's *Folklore.* "The song is about a lost romance and why young love is often fixed so permanently within our memories. Why it leaves such an indelible mark," she said in a live Twitter Q&A in 2020, alluding to the Betty/James/Inez mythology on the album. Some fans have a different take, though, interpreting it as a fan-appreciation song and adopting it as such. The lyrics "And when I felt like I was an old cardigan under someone's bed / You put me on and said I was your favorite" could well allude to her fans' fidelity through good times and bad.

Attending the 2013
Met Ball "PUNK:
Chaos to Couture."

Bleachella walks the press line at the 64th Annual BMI Pop Awards in 2016.

aesthetic; the kohl-black eye makeup and nude lips gave it massive edge. Returning to her romantic roots in 2014, she wore a gorgeous blush pink Oscar de la Renta gown with a dramatic train that nodded to her classic old Hollywood style influences. She was the cohost of the 2016 Met Gala, "Manus x Machina: Fashion in an Age of Technology." Her high-concept look there was one for the ages, a *Blade Runner*–esque ensemble from Louis Vuitton styled with platinum-blonde hair and black lipstick.

To paraphrase from her song "Bejeweled," she polishes up real nice. But she's just as comfortable in sweats and T-shirts—particularly if they have cats on them, as astute Swifties can attest. Like most people, she's more likely to be in cutoffs and a sweatshirt than a sparkly gown. For Taylor, comfort is king no matter what the occasion. "For me, it's important to be comfortable in what I'm wearing," she told *ASOS* magazine. "Being comfortable means that no one's going to be able to pull a fast one and take a picture of me that they'll deem to be embarrassing. I don't want to wear something so short that I'm scared there will be a wardrobe

> "Fashion is all about playful experimentation. If you don't look back at pictures of some of your old looks and cringe, you're doing it wrong. See: Bleachella."
>
> —TAYLOR TO *ELLE*

malfunction, or have a picture of me falling out of my shorts or skirt."

"Style is such a personal thing; it's your way to be an individual," she once tweeted.

The fact of the matter is that Taylor has always played with fashion because it's fun. Look no further than her music videos, where she plays dress-up constantly, often trying on multiple characters in one shoot. Followers of her socials also know how much she loves a costume party.

At the end of the day, all those fancy clothes are just part of the job. As Taylor told *Esquire* in 2014, "Music is the only thing that's ever fit me like that little black dress you wear every single time you go out." •

FIFTY SHADES OF TAY

A seasoned red-carpet veteran, Taylor has worn practically every hue imaginable. Here's a roundup of some of her best looks, in every color of the rainbow.

In Novis (2014)

In The Blonds (2022)

In Saint Laurent, IRO, and Kat Maconie (2019)

In Elie Saab (2012)

In Elie Saab (2015)

In Roberto Cavalli (2023)

In Raisa & Vanessa (2022)

Chapter Ten
THE OVERACHIEVER

Taylor won a staggering eight Billboard Music Awards in 2013 for her work on *Red*.

A self-described overachiever, there is not a facet of Taylor's career that she is not involved in. She sings. She writes. She produces. Heck, she even directs her own music videos. That's an impressive feat for anyone. Considering her unprecedented success, it's nothing short of staggering.

A list of Taylor's superlatives would fill this entire book and then some—and is ever growing—but here's a rundown of some of her major awards, as of 2023.

Grammy Awards: 46 nominations, 12 wins. That includes three Album of the Year awards and six Song of the Year nominations.

MTV Video Music Awards: 42 nominations and 14 wins, including three times for Video of the Year for "You Belong with Me," "Bad Blood," and "All Too Well (10 Minute Version)." Her 14 wins make her the fourth-most-decorated VMAs artist of all time.

American Music Awards: Taylor is the most awarded artist of all time at the AMAs, with 40 wins, including 7 Artist of the Year honors.

12

As of 2023, Taylor has been nominated for 46 Grammys and won 12, making her one of the most decorated female artists in Grammy history. She's also the only female solo artist to have won Album of the Year honors three times, for *Fearless*, *1989*, and *Folklore*.

Billboard Music Awards: Taylor has 29 BBMAs, the second-most in Billboard's history, behind only Drake.

Country Music Awards: While she may not be considered a country artist anymore, she's still getting attention from the Country Music Association, nabbing a nomination for a re-recorded track from *Red* that she released, featuring Chris Stapleton. Altogether Taylor has 10 CMAs, the most prestigious honor in country music.

Billboard named Taylor their first-ever Woman of the Decade in 2019, calling her "one of the most accomplished artists of all time." Announcing her honor, it wrote, "Swift has landed countless professional achievements.... The singer-songwriter is also being honored for her commitment to protecting creative rights, music education, literacy programs, cancer research, disaster relief, and the Time's Up initiative." She was also named Songwriter-Artist of the Decade by the Nashville Songwriters Association International and Artist of the Decade by the AMAs.

Taylor's so hardworking, it feels like there could be three of her.

She's also earned recognition for her advocacy work from a number of nonprofit organizations. She was given the Vanguard Award from GLAAD and an Attitude Icon Award for her LGBTQ advocacy work. "Everyone should be able to live out their love story without fear of discrimination," Taylor said in her Icon Award acceptance speech.

She's directed nine of her own music videos, including "ME!," "Anti-Hero," and "The Man," in which Taylor, in drag, answers her own musical question, experiencing what it would feel like to walk the world as a man.

Taylor went behind the camera to direct the film that accompanies the 10-minute version of "All Too Well," a longtime fan favorite from *Red* that was never released as a single. The short film premiered at the prestigious Tribeca Film Festival. *NME* wrote that the film "highlights the emotional power of [Swift's] unrivalled storytelling. That's in part thanks to some electric performances from *Stranger Things'* Sadie Sink and *Maze Runner's* Dylan O'Brien, but it would be nothing without the vulnerable creativity of the songwriter herself, who also wrote the story for the short." Taylor won a Grammy in 2023 for her direction.

The overwhelming response to the short film may have Taylor setting her sights even higher someday. "It would be so fantastic to write and direct…a feature," Taylor told *Variety* in 2022. "I don't see it being bigger,

EGOT THIS, TAYLOR!

She's won more music awards than anyone could ever count. But can she join the esteemed ranks of EGOTs? (Credit goes to *30 Rock* for the acronym; that's an individual who's won an Emmy, Grammy, Oscar, and Tony.) She's got armloads of Grammys, as well as an Emmy for her work on *AMEX Unstaged: Taylor Swift Experience*. A frequent contributor to films, an original song Oscar may well be in the cards someday. And she's already proven her mettle in musical theater, including the film adaptation of Andrew Lloyd Weber's *Cats*. Could Broadway be far behind?

in terms of scale. I loved making a film that was so intimate." To be sure, intimacy is Taylor's brand.

In front of the lens, she's even dabbled in acting, guest-starring on TV shows *CSI* and *The New Girl* and appearing in Hollywood movies including *Valentine's Day*, *The Giver*, and most recently David O. Russell's *Amsterdam* (2022). She also delivered purr-fection in the screen adaptation of Andrew Lloyd Weber's beloved musical *Cats*, performing "Macavity the Mystery Cat" as character Bombalurina.

Given Taylor's track record, where she will go next is anyone's guess. When she muses about her future, she's even said that she may just sunset being a performer and write songs for other artists. If anything is proven, it's that she's focused, thoughtful, and determined to give her best effort. Whatever she tries her hand at next, odds are she'll succeed. •

HIT**STORY**: "Blank Space"

It's one of Taylor's most popular songs of all time, a fizzy earworm (with a cheeky music video to match) that spent seven weeks at No. 1 on the Billboard charts (her best until 2022's "Anti-Hero" took that crown). It was a song she never intended to write but one that forced its way out of her. "I started writing it as a joke," she told SiriusXM in 2014. "I was…thinking about how the media has had a field day talking about what they think my personal life is like.… They've drawn up this fictitious profile of this girl who is a serial dater…overemotional…unstable, completely clingy, needy, like a nightmare.… And I just thought how incredibly complex and interesting that character actually is if [she] were a real girl and what kind of song she would write." Who said nothing good ever came out of tabloid journalism?

T.S. Blank Space

Boys only want love if it's torture.

Wearing Oscar
de la Renta at
the *Cats* movie
premiere in
2019.

"Writing songs is a calling, and getting to call it your career makes you very lucky. You have to be grateful every day for it and for all the people who thought your words might be worth listening to."

—TAYLOR IN 2022